HARNESSING THE

POWER

OF

TENSION

STRETCHED BUT NOT BROKEN

STUDY GUIDE

HARNESSING THE

POWER

OF

TENSION

STRETCHED BUT NOT BROKEN

SAMUEL R. CHAND

STUDY GUIDE

AVAIL

CONTENTS

Chapter 1. Tensions in Your Personal Life 6

Chapter 2. Tensions with People 14

Chapter 3. You Can't Escape It 22

Chapter 4. It's Your Choice 30

Chapter 5. Tensions in Implementation 38

Chapter 6. Tensions with the Vision 46

Chapter 7. Tensions When Facing Hard Choices 54

Chapter 8. Tensions in Communication 62

Chapter 9. Managing Tension (Before It Manages You!) .. 70

Chapter 10. New Expectations, Different Results 78

chapter 1

Tensions in Your Personal Life

"Some of us have devoted our lives to help others grow, but too often, we do little if anything to promote our own development."

Read Chapter 1 in *Harnessing the Power of Tension*. Use the Notes space to record any thoughts you want to remember or questions you want to talk about later.

Opening Thoughts

Home is a City of Refuge

- I need a guard rail
Healthy Rhythm
Work, Life Balance
Healthy Culture
Cultural Connection

In your personal life, what are some of the warning signs that you're "running on empty"?

REFLECT ON

Read Philippians 3:1-14:

"Further, my brothers and sisters, rejoice in the Lord! It is no trouble for me to write the same things to you again, and it is a safeguard for you. Watch out for those dogs, those evil-doers, those mutilators of the flesh. For it is we who are the circumcision, we who serve God by his Spirit, who boast in Christ Jesus, and who put no confidence in the flesh—though I myself have reasons for such confidence.

If someone else thinks they have reasons to put confidence in the flesh, I have more: circumcised on the eighth day, of the people of Israel, of the tribe of Benjamin, a Hebrew of Hebrews; in regard to the law, a Pharisee; as for zeal, persecuting the church; as for righteousness based on the law, faultless.

But whatever were gains to me I now consider loss for the sake of Christ. What is more, I consider everything a loss because of the surpassing worth of knowing Christ Jesus my Lord, for whose sake I have lost all things. I consider them garbage, that I may gain Christ and be found in him, not having a righteousness of my own that comes from the law, but that which is through faith in Christ—the righteousness that comes from God on the basis of faith. I want to know Christ—yes, to know the power of his resurrection and par-ticipation in his sufferings, becoming like him in his death, and so, somehow, attaining to the resurrection from the dead.

Not that I have already obtained all this, or have already arrived at my goal, but I press on to take hold of that for which Christ Jesus took hold of me. Brothers and sisters, I do not consider myself yet to have taken hold of it. But one thing I do: Forgetting what is behind and straining toward what is ahead, I press on toward the goal to win the prize for which God has called me heavenward in Christ Jesus."

What activities or practices help you refuel and refocus?

Invest In my Self
A Bigger Yes for my self

- Physical
- Social / Emotional
- Mental
- Spritually

Why do you think it's significant that Paul lists all of his accomplishments "in the flesh" first?

What fill's my tank

How does this perspective fly in the face of our worldly culture today? What difference is there in the message of this passage and the messages leaders receive every day in our industries?

"The tension is to give enough focus to the primary gift so we aren't distracted by the many gifts."

What gift(s) have you discovered in yourself, based on your own exploration and others' input?

_____

_____

_____

_____

_____

_____

How can you practically develop your gifts? What are specific steps you can take to hone your skills?

_____

_____

_____

_____

_____

_____

Have you found ways to deploy, or activate, your gift(s) to make a difference in your environment? What are some ideas for how you can do this?

_____

_____

_____

_____

_____

_____

In your own words, explain why tension in one area of life affects the rest of our lives as well.

_____

_____

_____

_____

_____

_____

What power and freedom comes from accepting tension as a reality of life? Are there any areas of your life in which you currently struggle to accept tension?

_____

_____

_____

_____

_____

_____

_____

Today, how would you describe your *tank, battery,* or *bank balance*? How "filled up" are you?

_____

_____

_____

_____

_____

_____

How can we live in the tension between success and fulfillment? Why is it important to have both operating in our lives?

_____

_____

_____

_____

_____

_____

_____

chapter 2

Tensions with People

"To the degree our connections with people are life-giving, we thrive; to the extent they drain us or harm us, we wilt."

Read Chapter 2 in *Harnessing the Power of Tension*. Use the Notes space to record any thoughts you want to remember or questions you want to talk about later.

Opening Thoughts

_____

_____

_____

_____

_____

_____

_____

In your current day-to-day life, what has been the most prevalent tension when it comes to your relationships?

_____

_____

_____

_____

_____

_____

REFLECT ON

Read Matthew 10:1-8, 34-39:

"Jesus called his twelve disciples to him and gave them authority to drive out impure spirits and to heal every disease and sickness.

These are the names of the twelve apostles: first, Simon (who is called Peter) and his brother Andrew; James son of Zebedee, and his brother John; Philip and Bartholomew; Thomas and Matthew the tax collector; James son of Alphaeus, and Thaddaeus; Simon the Zealot and Judas Iscariot, who betrayed him.

These twelve Jesus sent out with the following instructions: 'Do not go among the Gentiles or enter any town of the Samaritans. Go rather to the lost sheep of Israel. As you go, proclaim this message: "The kingdom of heaven has come near." Heal the sick, raise the dead, cleanse those who have leprosy, drive out demons. Freely you have received; freely give.

Do not suppose that I have come to bring peace to the earth. I did not come to bring peace, but a sword. For I have come to turn

"a man against his father,
   a daughter against her mother,
a daughter-in-law against her mother-in-law—
   a man's enemies will be the members of his own household."

Anyone who loves their father or mother more than me is not worthy of me; anyone who loves their son or daughter more than me is not worthy of me. Whoever does not take up their cross and follow me is not worthy of me. Whoever finds their life will lose it, and whoever loses their life for my sake will find it.'"

What has been the biggest benefit that your relationships have brought you lately?

_____

_____

_____

_____

_____

_____

_____

What examples of delegated, or borrowed, authority do you see in this passage?

_____

_____

_____

_____

_____

_____

What submission did the disciples need to exercise in order to wield this authority?

_____

_____

_____

_____

_____

_____

_____

SHARE YOUR STORY

"All of us have the opportunity to pour ourselves into the lives of others with a specific goal of helping them to have an ongoing impact. From person to person, we pay it forward and see lives changed."

What are some specific ways you can tailor your leadership to fit the needs of each person on your team? Think about the ways in which they are motivated, how they work, and how they interact with others.

_____
_____
_____
_____
_____

Explain the importance of balancing challenge with affirmation. What happens if you lean too far towards either end of the spectrum?

_____
_____
_____
_____
_____

How is voicing disagreement different from disunity? How do you recognize disunity on your team when it arises?

_____
_____
_____
_____
_____

What benefits has healthy disagreement brought to your team and even to your own personal leadership journey?

_____

_____

_____

_____

_____

_____

_____

In your own words, how would you explain the connections between systems and staff? How does each contribute to the other?

_____

_____

_____

_____

_____

_____

_____

Do you find yourself in a place where you can shepherd those you lead? Or has your organization grown so large that you've had to delegate shepherding responsibilities? How can you tell?

_____

_____

_____

_____

_____

_____

_____

Of the three options for acting on tension (embrace it, resolve it, or use it) which option do you find yourself utilizing most often? Is there an option you haven't utilized as much as you should?

_____

_____

_____

_____

_____

_____

_____

chapter 3

You Can't Escape It

"If we believe that the optimum life should be completely devoid of tension, we'll be confused, disappointed, and resentful of those people and events that disrupt our perfect peace. As leaders and parents, our goal isn't to relieve all tension, but instead to use it constructively."

READING TIME

Read Chapter 3 in *Harnessing the Power of Tension*. Use the Notes space to record any thoughts you want to remember or questions you want to talk about later.

Opening Thoughts

_____

_____

_____

_____

_____

_____

_____

Do you tend to get defensive when you sense tension on your team, or reflective? Explain your answer.

_____

_____

_____

_____

_____

_____

REFLECT ON

Read Proverbs 15:1-18:

"A gentle answer turns away wrath,
  but a harsh word stirs up anger.
The tongue of the wise adorns knowledge,
  but the mouth of the fool gushes folly.
The eyes of the LORD are everywhere,
  keeping watch on the wicked and the good.
The soothing tongue is a tree of life,
  but a perverse tongue crushes the spirit.
A fool spurns a parent's discipline,
  but whoever heeds correction shows prudence.
The house of the righteous contains great treasure,
  but the income of the wicked brings ruin.
The lips of the wise spread knowledge,
  but the hearts of fools are not upright.
The LORD detests the sacrifice of the wicked,
  but the prayer of the upright pleases him.
The LORD detests the way of the wicked,
  but he loves those who pursue righteousness.
Stern discipline awaits anyone who leaves the path;
  the one who hates correction will die.
Death and Destruction lie open before the LORD—
  how much more do human hearts!
Mockers resent correction,
  so they avoid the wise.
A happy heart makes the face cheerful,
  but heartache crushes the spirit.
The discerning heart seeks knowledge,
  but the mouth of a fool feeds on folly.
All the days of the oppressed are wretched,
  but the cheerful heart has a continual feast.
Better a little with the fear of the LORD
  than great wealth with turmoil.
Better a small serving of vegetables with love
  than a fattened calf with hatred.
A hot-tempered person stirs up conflict,
  but the one who is patient calms a quarrel."

What do you think is the underlying cause of your response? For example, if you feel defensive when tension arises, what beliefs or preconceptions about the tension may be contributing to that feeling?

_____

_____

_____

_____

_____

_____

What verses stand out most to you in this passage about handling tension? Write out your favorite 1-2 sentences below.

_____

_____

_____

_____

_____

_____

Looking at the way you personally handle tension, what needs to change according to the verses you wrote above? How can you ask God for help to better handle tensions as they arise?

_____

_____

_____

_____

_____

What's the difference between accepting the inevitability of tension and passively refusing to deal with it?

_____

_____

_____

_____

_____

_____

_____

How have you experienced tension in your familial relationships, or with a significant other?

_____

_____

_____

_____

_____

Why do you think even positive life events have a high capacity for tension? Have you experienced any of these "high-tension" positive events?

_____

_____

_____

_____

_____

_____

How have you experienced tension in your work or church relationships?

_____

_____

_____

_____

_____

Do you personally find it easy or difficult to come to grips with the presence of tension? Explain your answer.

_____

_____

_____

_____

_____

How has tension caused change for the better in you personally? How have you grown from dealing with it?

_____

_____

_____

_____

_____

What potential does tension hold for improving your team, both as individuals and as a whole?

_____

_____

_____

_____

_____

chapter 4

It's Your Choice

"If our hope is to see God use the tension to produce something good, something noble, and something of lasting value, we can have assurance that He will come through…in His way…and in His timing."

READING TIME

Read Chapter 4 in *Harnessing the Power of Tension.* Use the Notes space to record any thoughts you want to remember or questions you want to talk about later.

Opening Thoughts

_____

_____

_____

_____

_____

_____

_____

_____

_____

_____

Do you find it easy to look at tension in a positive light? Why or why not?

_____

_____

_____

_____

_____

REFLECT ON

Read James 1:2-18:

"Count it all joy, my brothers, when you meet trials of various kinds, for you know that the testing of your faith produces steadfastness. And let steadfastness have its full effect, that you may be perfect and complete, lacking in nothing.

If any of you lacks wisdom, let him ask God, who gives generously to all without reproach, and it will be given him. But let him ask in faith, with no doubting, for the one who doubts is like a wave of the sea that is driven and tossed by the wind. For that person must not suppose that he will receive anything from the Lord; he is a double-minded man, unstable in all his ways.

Let the lowly brother boast in his exaltation, and the rich in his humiliation, because like a flower of the grass he will pass away. For the sun rises with its scorching heat and withers the grass; its flower falls, and its beauty perishes. So also will the rich man fade away in the midst of his pursuits.

Blessed is the man who remains steadfast under trial, for when he has stood the test he will receive the crown of life, which God has promised to those who love him. Let no one say when he is tempted, 'I am being tempted by God,' for God cannot be tempted with evil, and he himself tempts no one. But each person is tempted when he is lured and enticed by his own desire. Then desire when it has conceived gives birth to sin, and sin when it is fully grown brings forth death.

Do not be deceived, my beloved brothers. Every good gift and every perfect gift is from above, coming down from the Father of lights, with whom there is no variation or shadow due to change. Of his own will he brought us forth by the word of truth, that we should be a kind of firstfruits of his creatures."

Are there any tensions in your life currently that are growing and maturing you as a leader? What are they?

_____

_____

_____

_____

_____

_____

_____

How does James's viewpoint on suffering differ from today's American perspective?

_____

_____

_____

_____

_____

_____

_____

What rewards and enrichments does James list for those who endure challenge, tension, and hardship for the sake of their God-given calling?

_____

_____

_____

_____

_____

_____

_____

Explain the difference between a tension that destroys and a tension that strengthens. Do you have any instances of either kind of tension in your life right now?

_____

_____

_____

_____

_____

_____

Why is it dangerous to oversimplify the intricate issues of tension? What do we potentially miss out on when we do this?

_____

_____

_____

_____

_____

How did Jesus's approach to tension differ from the approach (or avoidance) that we often use?

_____

_____

_____

_____

_____

What specific tensions does your organization face that are unique to your industry (business tensions, ministry tensions, etc.)?

_____

_____

_____

_____

_____

What are some practical ways in which can you help make tension—and even failure—something that your team is able to talk about freely?

_____

_____

_____

_____

_____

Do you find it easy to be honest about your own personal tensions? Why or why not?

_____

_____

_____

_____

_____

How can you apply what you've learned this chapter to the tensions in your life?

_____

_____

_____

_____

chapter 5

Tensions in Implementation

"Implementing an idea is much more than the leader articulating a glowing image of what can be; it requires the details of planning, delegation, and feedback that are essential to success."

READING TIME

Read Chapter 5 in *Harnessing the Power of Tension*. Use the Notes space to record any thoughts you want to remember or questions you want to talk about later.

Opening Thoughts

_____

_____

_____

_____

_____

_____

_____

What tensions have you encountered as you seek to delegate and implement new things in your organization?

_____

_____

_____

_____

_____

_____

REFLECT ON

Read Exodus 18:13-27:

"The next day Moses sat to judge the people, and the people stood around Moses from morning till evening. When Moses' father-in-law saw all that he was doing for the people, he said, 'What is this that you are doing for the people? Why do you sit alone, and all the people stand around you from morning till evening?' And Moses said to his father-in-law, 'Because the people come to me to inquire of God; when they have a dispute, they come to me and I decide between one person and another, and I make them know the statutes of God and his laws.' Moses' father-in-law said to him, 'What you are doing is not good. You and the people with you will certainly wear yourselves out, for the thing is too heavy for you. You are not able to do it alone. Now obey my voice; I will give you advice, and God be with you! You shall represent the people before God and bring their cases to God, and you shall warn them about the statutes and the laws, and make them know the way in which they must walk and what they must do. Moreover, look for able men from all the people, men who fear God, who are trustworthy and hate a bribe, and place such men over the people as chiefs of thousands, of hundreds, of fifties, and of tens. And let them judge the people at all times. Every great matter they shall bring to you, but any small matter they shall decide themselves. So it will be easier for you, and they will bear the burden with you. If you do this, God will direct you, you will be able to endure, and all this people also will go to their place in peace.'

So Moses listened to the voice of his father-in-law and did all that he had said. Moses chose able men out of all Israel and made them heads over the people, chiefs of thousands, of hundreds, of fifties, and of tens. And they judged the people at all times. Any hard case they brought to Moses, but any small matter they decided themselves. Then Moses let his father-in-law depart, and he went away to his own country."

How is it sometimes easier to just attempt to do it all yourself? How does this make your role more difficult? How does it handicap your team?

_____

_____

_____

_____

_____

_____

What criteria did Jethro require for the men who would take over responsibility from Moses?

_____

_____

_____

_____

_____

_____

What criteria do you need to seek for those you delegate to in your organization?

_____

_____

_____

_____

_____

_____

Recall a time you delegated an important responsibility to another team member. What was difficult about doing this? How did it free you up as a leader?

_____

_____

_____

_____

_____

Explain the difference between abstract and concrete language. Which do you excel in naturally? How can you bridge the gap between your kind of language and those on the team who don't share it as much?

_____

_____

_____

_____

_____

_____

Which of the bulleted questions in this chapter (about delegating) stood out to you the most? Which questions do you need to ask yourself more on a daily basis?

_____

_____

_____

_____

_____

What are some practical actions, resources, or relationships you can invest in to keep learning and growing as a leader?

_____

_____

_____

_____

_____

How has your upbringing, and the individuals in your life to date, influenced the words, tone, actions, and attitudes you hold today? What's positive about these influences? What are some things you'd rather leave behind from them?

_____

_____

_____

_____

_____

Explain the difference between spending time and investing time as a leader. Why is the latter more effective for both you and your team?

_____

_____

_____

_____

_____

_____

_____

What are some concrete ways you can seek intuition and advice from those on your team?

_____

_____

_____

_____

_____

_____

How can you celebrate incremental successes right now in your organization? What will this do for team morale and performance?

_____

_____

_____

_____

_____

_____

chapter 6

Tensions with the Vision

"To lead any kind of genuine change, we have to live in the tension between the lessons we've internalized in the past and the path to new horizons."

READING TIME

Read Chapter 6 in *Harnessing the Power of Tension.* Use the Notes space to record any thoughts you want to remember or questions you want to talk about later.

Opening Thoughts

_____

_____

_____

_____

_____

_____

_____

_____

What are some of the tensions you've encountered as you strive to move toward your vision?

_____

_____

_____

_____

_____

REFLECT ON

Read Acts 6:1-7:

"Now in these days when the disciples were increasing in number, a complaint by the Hellenists arose against the Hebrews because their widows were being neglected in the daily distribution. And the twelve summoned the full number of the disciples and said, 'It is not right that we should give up preaching the word of God to serve tables. Therefore, brothers, pick out from among you seven men of good repute, full of the Spirit and of wisdom, whom we will appoint to this duty. But we will devote ourselves to prayer and to the ministry of the word.' And what they said pleased the whole gathering, and they chose Stephen, a man full of faith and of the Holy Spirit, and Philip, and Prochorus, and Nicanor, and Timon, and Parmenas, and Nicolaus, a proselyte of Antioch. These they set before the apostles, and they prayed and laid their hands on them.

And the word of God continued to increase, and the number of the disciples multiplied greatly in Jerusalem, and a great many of the priests became obedient to the faith."

How have tensions in your organization's past contributed to your systems and structures today?

_____

_____

_____

_____

_____

_____

How did the twelve apostles show flexibility in this situation?

_____

_____

_____

_____

_____

_____

_____

How did the twelve apostles show inflexibility, or commitment to certain systems and structures, in this situation?

_____

_____

_____

_____

_____

_____

_____

*"All strategic
plans should
be written
in pencil.
The organi-
zations that
are too rigid
miss oppor-
tunities, are
often con-
fused when
they fall
behind, and
need to find
someone
to blame.
Planning
certainly is
necessary,
but it's
important
to keep our
eyes open to
new oppor-
tunities."*

Do you tend to write your strategic plans in pen, or in pencil? Explain your answer.

_____

_____

_____

_____

_____

_____

_____

How does flow benefit a leader as he or she pursues the vision? What benefit do systems and structures bring? In your own words, explain how the two work together in your leadership.

_____

_____

_____

_____

_____

What are the dangers of operating too much in flow?

_____

_____

_____

_____

_____

_____

What are the dangers of relying too heavily on systems and structures?

_____

_____

_____

_____

List some things that have worked well for you in the past, but that won't work as you move forward.

_____

_____

_____

_____

_____

What new systems and structures will be required as you step into your future?

_____

_____

_____

_____

_____

How do you determine whether or not a risk is one that will serve your company's mission?

_____

_____

_____

_____

_____

chapter 7

Tensions When Facing Hard Choices

"All men are created equal"—but our decisions aren't.

READING TIME

Read Chapter 7 in *Harnessing the Power of Tension*. Use the Notes space to record any thoughts you want to remember or questions you want to talk about later.

Opening Thoughts

_____

_____

_____

_____

_____

_____

_____

What difficult decisions have arisen in your leadership recently? What tensions have these decisions brought to both you and your team?

_____

_____

_____

_____

_____

REFLECT ON

Read Mark 10:35-45:

"And James and John, the sons of Zebedee, came up to him and said to him, 'Teacher, we want you to do for us whatever we ask of you.' And he said to them, 'What do you want me to do for you?' And they said to him, 'Grant us to sit, one at your right hand and one at your left, in your glory.' Jesus said to them, 'You do not know what you are asking. Are you able to drink the cup that I drink, or to be baptized with the baptism with which I am baptized?' And they said to him, 'We are able.' And Jesus said to them, 'The cup that I drink you will drink, and with the baptism with which I am baptized, you will be baptized, but to sit at my right hand or at my left is not mine to grant, but it is for those for whom it has been prepared.' And when the ten heard it, they began to be indignant at James and John. And Jesus called them to him and said to them, 'You know that those who are considered rulers of the Gentiles lord it over them, and their great ones exercise authority over them. But it shall not be so among you. But whoever would be great among you must be your servant, and whoever would be first among you must be slave of all. For even the Son of Man came not to be served but to serve, and to give his life as a ransom for many.'"

How did James and John misinterpret the kind of leadership Jesus came to demonstrate?

_____

_____

_____

_____

_____

_____

How do you see Jesus acting as both shepherd and CEO of his disciples in this passage?

_____

_____

_____

_____

_____

_____

_____

What is your biggest takeaway from this passage?

_____

_____

_____

_____

_____

_____

_____

SHARE
YOUR
STORY

*"The tension
between big
and little
decisions
is one most
of us don't
think about,
but if we do,
we'll spend
more time
making sure
we get the
big ones
right."*

In your own words, explain each of the four stages of competence, and what strengths/ weaknesses they each pose.

_____
_____
_____
_____
_____
_____

Have you had to give up any "shepherding" responsibilities as your organization has grown? How has your relationship to your congregation or customer base changed over the course of your organization's lifetime?

_____
_____
_____

How have your responsibilities overlapped in terms of being a leader, a pastor, an executive, a guide, etc.? What tensions have you encountered in negotiating a balance among your various roles?

_____
_____
_____
_____
_____

What details, solutions, or problems seem obvious to you but to which your team is largely oblivious?

_____

_____

_____

_____

_____

_____

_____

How can you challenge your team to acknowledge and recognize these things? Conversely, how can you value their unique perspectives and the way they notice things that you don't see?

_____

_____

_____

_____

_____

_____

_____

Explain the connection between leadership and service. How can you better serve those under your leadership? Get specific here.

_____

_____

_____

_____

_____

_____

_____

Would you consider yourself "comfortable in ambiguity"? Do you like to provide clarity or comfort more? Explain your answers.

_____

_____

_____

_____

_____

_____

_____

chapter 8

Tensions in Communication

*"Damage can happen if leaders communicate
too much too soon to too many."*

READING TIME

Read Chapter 8 in *Harnessing the Power of Tension*. Use the Notes space to record any thoughts you want to remember or questions you want to talk about later.

Opening Thoughts

_____

_____

_____

_____

_____

_____

_____

_____

How do you currently strategize, or cascade, important communications in your organization? Who hears first, second, third…last?

_____

_____

_____

_____

_____

REFLECT ON

Read Ephesians 4:11-16:

"And he gave the apostles, the prophets, the evangelists, the shepherds and teachers, to equip the saints for the work of ministry, for building up the body of Christ, until we all attain to the unity of the faith and of the knowledge of the Son of God, to mature manhood, to the measure of the stature of the fullness of Christ, so that we may no longer be children, tossed to and fro by the waves and carried about by every wind of doctrine, by human cunning, by craftiness in deceitful schemes. Rather, speaking the truth in love, we are to grow up in every way into him who is the head, into Christ, from whom the whole body, joined and held together by every joint with which it is equipped, when each part is working properly, makes the body grow so that it builds itself up in love."

How does your communication to each of the groups you listed above differ? For instance, what details do you share with some groups that you don't share with others?

_____

_____

_____

_____

_____

_____

What balance does this passage require between truth and love? How can you as a leader express both of these things at the same time?

_____

_____

_____

_____

_____

_____

How do different members of your team model truth and love to you? How have you learned from their examples?

_____

_____

_____

_____

_____

_____

Which steps from Sam's ten-step communication cascading plan stood out the most to you? Which do you need to implement in your own communication strategy?

_____

_____

_____

_____

_____

_____

_____

In your own words, what does it mean for a vision to:

Synergize? _____

_____

Galvanize? _____

_____

Energize? _____

_____

Do you resonate with the generational differences presented in this chapter? Which of these distinct perspectives have you noticed in your own team?

_____

_____

_____

_____

_____

_____

What are you currently doing to bridge the gaps between generations on your team? What steps do you want to begin taking in the future ?

_____

_____

_____

_____

_____

In what ways are you a "silent leader"? In what ways are you a "vocal leader"?

_____

_____

_____

_____

_____

How do you know when it's time to speak up and when it's time to stay silent? How do you read the room to figure this out?

_____

_____

_____

_____

_____

How can you carve out time in your day for silence? Be specific!

_____

_____

_____

_____

_____

chapter 9

Managing Tension
(Before It Manages You!)

"It is inherent in the role of leadership to create tension. By definition, leaders take people to places that are unfamiliar, often uncomfortable, and even threatening. We might even say that the first job of a great leader is to increase the level of stress."

Read Chapter 9 in *Harnessing the Power of Tension*. Use the Notes space to record any thoughts you want to remember or questions you want to talk about later.

Opening Thoughts

_____

_____

_____

_____

_____

_____

_____

Do you send the message to your team that you're afraid of tension? Or do you proactively encourage your team to embrace and even seek out healthy tension?

_____

_____

_____

_____

_____

REFLECT ON

Read Leviticus 23:33-44:

"And the LORD spoke to Moses, saying, 'Speak to the people of Israel, saying, On the fifteenth day of this seventh month and for seven days is the Feast of Booths to the LORD. On the first day shall be a holy convocation; you shall not do any ordinary work. For seven days you shall present food offerings to the LORD. On the eighth day you shall hold a holy convocation and present a food offering to the LORD. It is a solemn assembly; you shall not do any ordinary work.

'These are the appointed feasts of the LORD, which you shall proclaim as times of holy convocation, for presenting to the LORD food offerings, burnt offerings and grain offerings, sacrifices and drink offerings, each on its proper day, besides the LORD's Sabbaths and besides your gifts and besides all your vow offerings and besides all your freewill offerings, which you give to the LORD.

'On the fifteenth day of the seventh month, when you have gathered in the produce of the land, you shall celebrate the feast of the LORD seven days. On the first day shall be a solemn rest, and on the eighth day shall be a solemn rest. And you shall take on the first day the fruit of splendid trees, branches of palm trees and boughs of leafy trees and willows of the brook, and you shall rejoice before the LORD your God seven days. You shall celebrate it as a feast to the LORD for seven days in the year. It is a statute forever throughout your generations; you shall celebrate it in the seventh month. You shall dwell in booths for seven days. All native Israelites shall dwell in booths, that your generations may know that I made the people of Israel dwell in booths when I brought them out of the land of Egypt: I am the LORD your God.'

Thus Moses declared to the people of Israel the appointed feasts of the LORD."

What does it do to our company culture when we send the message that tension is bad, to be feared, and to be avoided?

_____

_____

_____

_____

_____

_____

The Feast of Booths was only one of several annual feasts the Lord required His people to observe. Why do you think God made such a big deal out of regularly celebrating and resting?

_____

_____

_____

_____

_____

_____

How do you think this impacted the morale and attitude of the Israelite people? How have you seen celebration and rest impact the wellbeing of your own people?

_____

_____

_____

_____

_____

_____

What did you think of Dr. Chand's story about confronting conflict on the team during a meeting? Did you gain any insights from this account?

_____

_____

_____

_____

_____

_____

_____

_____

_____

_____

What's the difference between promoting tension that makes you the center of attention, and promoting tension that takes the attention off you and puts it onto a problem or opportunity?

_____

_____

_____

_____

_____

_____

_____

_____

_____

Look at the bulleted list of questions that people on teams ask about their leaders. How are you answering each of these questions today, right now, for your team?

_____

_____

_____

_____

_____

What's the difference between destructive and productive interpersonal tension? How can you tell the difference in your daily meetings and interactions with others?

_____

_____

_____

_____

_____

List some things that are currently working, or succeeding, in your organization. How can you celebrate these things with your team this week?

_____

_____

_____

_____

_____

Of the three kinds of tension listed in this chapter (tension to be resolved, tension to be overlooked, and tension that's good and productive), which do you have the most of in your organization right now? How can you see each kind in the teams you work with today?

_____

_____

_____

_____

_____

Which "ropes" are you going to pick up right now as a leader? Which "ropes" are you going to leave on the ground today? Explain how you came to these conclusions.

_____

_____

_____

_____

_____

chapter 10

New Expectations, Different Results

"Focusing on what's wrong produces a toxic mixture of blame, shame, discouragement, and despair. The human heart thrives on hope, affirmation, and inspir ation."

_____

_____

_____

_____

_____

_____

_____

If you're honest with yourself, do you tend to focus more on blame and correction in your leadership, or hope and affirmation? How do you know?

_____

_____

_____

_____

REFLECT ON

Read John 21:15-25:

"When they had finished breakfast, Jesus said to Simon Peter, 'Simon, son of John, do you love me more than these?' He said to him, 'Yes, Lord; you know that I love you.' He said to him, 'Feed my lambs.' He said to him a second time, 'Simon, son of John, do you love me?' He said to him, 'Yes, Lord; you know that I love you.' He said to him, 'Tend my sheep.' He said to him the third time, 'Simon, son of John, do you love me?' Peter was grieved because he said to him the third time, 'Do you love me?' and he said to him, 'Lord, you know everything; you know that I love you.' Jesus said to him, 'Feed my sheep. Truly, truly, I say to you, when you were young, you used to dress yourself and walk wherever you wanted, but when you are old, you will stretch out your hands, and another will dress you and carry you where you do not want to go.' (This he said to show by what kind of death he was to glorify God.) And after saying this he said to him, 'Follow me.'

Peter turned and saw the disciple whom Jesus loved following them, the one who also had leaned back against him during the supper and had said, 'Lord, who is it that is going to betray you?' When Peter saw him, he said to Jesus, 'Lord, what about this man?' Jesus said to him, 'If it is my will that he remain until I come, what is that to you? You follow me!' So the saying spread abroad among the brothers that this disciple was not to die; yet Jesus did not say to him that he was not to die, but, 'If it is my will that he remain until I come, what is that to you?'

This is the disciple who is bearing witness about these things, and who has written these things, and we know that his testimony is true.

Now there are also many other things that Jesus did. Were every one of them to be written, I suppose that the world itself could not contain the books that would be written."

How are both of the above (correction and affirmation) necessary? How do you know when the occasion calls for correction?
Affirmation?

_____

_____

_____

_____

_____

_____

How does Jesus embrace and utilize tension in this passage? Why
do you think this was a necessary tension to address?

_____

_____

_____

_____

_____

_____

How does Jesus avoid and move away from tension in this passage?
Why do you think this was not a necessary tension to address?

_____

_____

_____

_____

_____

_____

How are you practically communicating your company values to employees and potential hires?

_____

_____

_____

_____

_____

_____

Have you prioritized your onboarding process to date? Why or why not? What do you need to add to make it as effective as possible in communicating your values, culture, and vision?

_____

_____

_____

_____

Look at the list of things you avoid by using tension. Which items stand out to you the most as things you need to do a better job of avoiding in your leadership?

_____

_____

_____

_____

_____

_____

Look at the list of things you gain by using tension. Which items stand out to you the most as things you need to do a better job of embracing in your leadership?

_____

_____

_____

_____

How can you know whether it's necessary to do an "autopsy" of a problem? What are some signs that it's only a distraction to you and your team?

_____

_____

_____

_____

_____

As you come to the end of this study, list below the top action steps, insights, and points that have impacted you the most.

_____

_____

_____

_____

If you had to summarize what God is calling you to do in terms of the tensions you face as a leader, how would you state it in one to two sentences?

_____

_____

_____

_____